IOANNIS VASILEIOU

PALOP-TL

....

THE PORTUGUESE-SPEAKING AFRICAN COUNTRIES AND TIMOR-LESTE

....

HISTORY-ECONOMY-TRADE

ATHENS 2019

ART DIRECTOR: SOFIA LIVIERATOU, sofialiv@hotmail.com

ACKNOWLEDGEMENTS
To my beloved father

TABLE OF CONTENTS

INTRODUCTION

The principal objective of this book is to meticulously examine the tremendously interesting in far too many senses "Países Africanos de Língua Oficial Portuguesa e Timor-Leste" (PALOP-TL) group. As we will see, the notability of this group and its member states in a global scale is incontrovertibly evident and, following our hitherto conducted research, we remain perfectly sure that it will be rapidly increased in the near future.

Portuguese is the official language of Angola, Cape Verde, Guinea-Bissau, Mozambique and Sao Tome and Principe. These countries are all located in Africa, whereas it is worth mentioning that the distance between some of them can irrefutably be regarded as enormous.

However, according to more than a few documents we have meticulously studied, one of our foremost conclusions is that such a factor is not in position to affect a great deal their truly multidimensional spectrum of relations.

So, the word PALOP stands for the member countries of the Portuguese-Speaking African Countries, while PALOP-TL became the group's name after Timor-Leste (which is located in Southeast Asia) became its 6th member back in 2007. Due to the fact that Portuguese is their official language, the five African PALOP-TL member states belong to "Lusophone Africa".

In March 1992, in Sao Tome, the heads of state and government of PALOP managed to express their will to create a number of highly notable cooperative relations both with the EU and with each other, including of course Timor-Leste from 2007. Therefore, the group was renamed PALOP-TL. The latter can unquestionably be regarded as an indisputably significant group due to numerous reasons which will be thoroughly examined in the following chapters.

A slightly strange element we have managed to discover in the context of our attempt to conscientiously scrutinize the already existing literature is that, despite its irrefutable noteworthiness, PALOP-TL has not yet been extensively analyzed. And we mean in the context of books and journal articles in English.

Of course we do not imply that the group has been deliberately ignored and this has to be made crystal clear from the very beginning. Nonetheless, taking the group's high significance into account, we expected to discover more material systematically coping with it.

In our opinion and always according to our findings, it would be much better if these countries could become a more popular subject in terms of economic studies. We remain perfectly sure that their painstaking examination would provide a wealth of knowledge and a sufficient explanation with respect not only to their current economic and financial situation but also to their future prospects.

We do not mean that the current book is the only one that meticulously presents and examines that kind of data, but we really hope that via this book PALOP-TL member countries will eventually receive a higher degree of attention with regard to their numerous tremendously significant attempts towards a more promising economic future.

However, a number of outstandingly notable articles by well-known scholars which have been published in some of the most prestigious journals worldwide incontrovertibly exist. These provide us with remarkable information as far as a wide range of attention-grabbing issues is concerned. Hence, a section of this book has been dedicated to the conscientious analysis of the work by Alao, Chabal, De Medeiros Carvalho, Galli, Hamilton and Moser.

In order to speak more generally, we have to note that in the context of this book we attempt to painstakingly examine a) the profiles of the six member countries of PALOP-TL, and b) the truly ambitious and incontrovertibly multifarious collaboration between PALOP-TL and the European Union (EU).

We remain certain that our analysis takes place in a well-organized and simplified manner with a view to a coherent understanding. The spectrum of our examination is indubitably broad and complicated, but we strongly believe that the method on which we have relied can make the reader become familiar with these matters without being tired or perplexed.

As we have already mentioned, some of the PALOP-TL member countries are not characterized by geographical proximity and especially when we refer to Timor-Leste, which also belongs to a different continent. What is more, even in the case of some of the African member states, we can undoubtedly observe the truly long distance between them.

Nonetheless, we surely have to note that this undeniably fruitful cooperation becomes a reality thanks to a highly notable cooperative spirit and due to specific cultural and historical bonds between the abovementioned countries.

A negative feature, though, in terms of all the PALOP-TL member states without a single exception is the tremendously high percentage of population below poverty line. Such an element is incontrovertibly gloomy and inevitably calls for further analysis and rapid action.

As we can easily understand, it is not easy for such a negative situation to be efficaciously confronted in the near future. Nevertheless we really hope that in the distant future a certain degree of progress with respect to this incontestably burning issue will somehow become a reality.

Apart from the introduction, this book comprises three more chapters. In Chapter 1, we systematically focus on the methodical presentation of *"The Profile of PALOP-TL's Six Member Countries"*. In this chapter we are based, inter alia, on numerous interesting quantitative data and try to provide the reader with the most recent and accurate information as regards history, geography, trade and economy of PALOP-TL member states emphasizing the most considerable elements.

Chapter 2, titled *"A Critical Comparison between PALOP-TL Members and the Cooperation with the European Union"* has been divided into three parts. Firstly, we attempt a critical comparison between the six PALOP-TL member countries, using the data which have been painstakingly presented in the context of the previous chapter. Our dominant aim is to point out the most notable similarities and differences that incontrovertibly exist between the six countries.

Secondly, we critically concentrate on a number of truly notable journal articles which have indeed managed to provide us with tremendously interesting information not only in terms of politics and economics but also with respect to history, culture and civilization in general.

Thirdly, we conscientiously scrutinize the foremost factors and parameters that more or less define the cooperation between PALOP-TL and the EU. As we will notice, this cooperation is unquestionably significant for both the present and the future, therefore, a thorough examination is absolutely essential.

Finally, in Chapter 3, the foremost *"Concluding Remarks"* are being carefully highlighted in order for a sufficient summary with regard to the key arguments on which this book has been based to become a reality.

In the context of that final chapter, the already achieved targets are being systematically underlined, the current difficulties are being methodically presented and the most notable future prospects are being conscientiously examined in order for the reader to be adequately provided with impetus for further research.

Nobody is in position to accurately predict the future and any attempts to do so will definitely sound utopian. Nevertheless, in the case of PALOP-TL it is true that numerous significant steps towards a more heartening future have incontestably taken place. Consequently, such an astounding feature indisputably sends positive messages and makes us believe that its already crucial role is highly likely to become much more pivotal in the context of (why not?) the international arena.

The fact that PALOP-TL is admittedly regarded as one of the most cohesive ACP groupings despite a) the numerous severe political and economic tribulations its member states have suffered and b) the already mentioned high percentage of population below poverty line irrefutably makes us more optimistic with regard to the future, as far as of course the majority of the actions planned become a reality in the required manner.

CHAPTER 1

THE PROFILE OF PALOP-TL'S SIX MEMBER COUNTRIES

In this chapter, our dominant objective is to conduct a scrupulous examination with regard to the historical, geographical, economic and trade profiles of the six PALOP-TL member countries. We would like to believe that our scrutiny and the subsequent analysis will offer the reader the coveted opportunity to discover a wealth of interesting information that are highly probable to lead him to the extraction of numerous notable conclusions.

In the first pages, we critically highlight some really noteworthy historical information as regards the six group members, while in the following ones we conscientiously present geographical information and quantitative data in the context of a wide array of highly important issues.

In addition to that, we have to note that the method of analysis on which this book is based is up to a point similar to the one we have already used in terms of a number of our previous books (Vasileiou, 2013a, 2014a, 2015, 2017c, 2018c, 2019a, 2019b, 2019f, 2019h, 2019j and 2019k).

With respect to the specific analysis of the historical information and as we will notice in the next paragraphs, it is irrefutably worth mentioning that all the PALOP-TL member states, from their independence onwards, have experienced several devastating political crises with a huge unpropitious impact. Therefore, it would not be an exaggeration to argue that the progress of this group can be characterized as more or less miraculous (Vasileiou, 2013a, 2014a, 2015, 2017c, 2018c, 2019a, 2019b, 2019f, 2019h, 2019j and 2019k).

It goes without saying that any negative situation that takes place in an individual country can indisputably affect the group as a whole and following our hitherto conducted research (not solely in the context of this book) we have already witnessed the precise consequences of such a phenomenon in far too many cases (Vasileiou, 2013a, 2014a, 2015, 2017c, 2018c, 2019a, 2019b, 2019f, 2019h, 2019j and 2019k).

What is more, always in our opinion, this argument becomes even stronger especially when the group in question consists only of six members and used to comprise just five until 2007 in the context of its previous form.

Our historical overview which also includes a number of attention-grabbing economic features begins with Angola, which became independent from Portugal in 1975.

After that, a catastrophic battle between the Jonas Savimbi's National Union for the Total Independence of Angola (UNITA) and the Jose Eduardo Dos Santos's Popular Movement for the

Liberation of Angola (MPLA) began. Such a calamitous situation almost resulted in total chaos. In 1992 peace seemed probable due to the fact that national elections in Angola became a reality. Regrettably, fighting commenced again in the following year and according to estimations up to 1.5 million people may have died and four million people may have been displaced in the dreadful context of more than 25 years of battling. In 2002, Savimbi died and 15 years later Dos Santos finally stepped down from the presidency, having been Angola's leader since 1979. This feature is far from insignificant since it adequately highlights the end of an era. In August 2017, Joao Lourenco was elected president (Alao, 1999; Chabal, 1996; CIA Factbook/Angola, 2019; De Medeiros Carvalho, 2015; Encyclopedia "Domi", Vol. 1; Encyclopedia "The Counselor of the Young", Vol. 1; Galli, 1987; Hamilton, 1991a and 1991b; Moser, 1999; Penvenne, 2003; Purnell History of the 20th Century, 1968, Vol 1 and 6; Vasileiou, 2019f; World History 1, 1990).

Cape Verde is the second step of our examination and we have to mention that it also became independent in 1975.

Following a certain interest with regard to unification with Guinea-Bissau, a specific one-party system was created and lasted until 1990 when multi-party elections took place. Its economy depends on foreign investment, tourism, development aid and remittances. Despite the fact that approximately 40% of the population lives in rural areas, the food production share in GDP can incontrovertibly be characterized as low.

Emphasis must also be placed on the fact that the dominant targets of economic reforms are to a) methodically decrease high unemployment, b) systematically develop the private sector and c) successfully attract foreign investment (Alao, 1999; Chabal, 1996; CIA Factbook/Cape Verde, 2019; De Medeiros Carvalho, 2015; Encyclopedia "The Counselor of the Young", Vol. 8; Galli, 1987; Hamilton, 1991a and 1991b; Moser, 1999; Penvenne, 2003; World History 2, 1990).

We continue with Guinea-Bissau, which became independent from Portugal one year earlier compared to the two abovementioned PALOP-TL members.

Regrettably, six years later, a military coup established General Joao Bernardo "Nino" Vieira as president, while it is worth mentioning that numerous coup attempts that took place during the 1980s and the early 1990s did not manage to unseat him. Eventually, in 1994, Vieira was elected president in the context of Guinea-Bissau's first free, multiparty election but due to a specific military mutiny that led to a nightmarish civil war in 1998, Vieira was ejected in May of the following year. Afterwards, Guinea-Bissau experienced far too many adverse political tribulations. In April 2018, a) a consensus prime minister was appointed, b) the national legislature which was closed for two years managed to open again and c) a new government became a reality under Prime Minister Aristides Gomes. Furthermore, we have to note that in March 2019, the government held legislative elections, voting in the PAIGC as the ruling party (Alao, 1999; Chabal, 1996; CIA Factbook/Guinea-Bissau, 2019; De Medeiros Carvalho, 2015; Encyclopedia "Domi", Vol. 7; Encyclopedia "The Counselor of the Young", Vol. 3; Galli, 1987; Hamilton, 1991a and 1991b; Moser, 1999; Penvenne, 2003; World History 1, 1990).

Mozambique is the fourth step of our analysis and just like Angola and Cape Verde it became independent from Portugal in 1975.

Unfortunately, numerous outstandingly unpleasant factors such as, inter alia, a) economic dependence on South Africa, b) a devastating civil war, c) a significant emigration and d) a harsh drought placed numerous insurmountable obstacles with regard to its development till the mid-1990s. As soon as independence became a reality Mozambique was one of the poorest countries worldwide. In 1987, the government commenced a number of highly significant macroeconomic reforms, the principal target of which was the much-needed economic stabilization. In addition to that, a number of notable fiscal reforms have incontrovertibly managed to substantially enhance the government's revenue collection abilities (Alao, 1999; Chabal, 1996; CIA Factbook/Mozambique, 2019; De Medeiros Carvalho, 2015; Encyclopedia "Domi", Vol. 18; Encyclopedia "The Counselor of the Young", Vol. 7; Galli, 1987; Hamilton, 1991a and 1991b; Moser, 1999; Penvenne, 2003; Purnell History of the 20th Century, 1968, Vol. 1, 2 and 6; Vasileiou, 2019f; World History 2, 1990).

Our examination continues with Sao Tome and Principe, which also became independent in 1975.

Nonetheless, it is worth mentioning that its first free elections became a reality only in 1991. It is essential to point out that a series of regular internal disputes between political parties in a sense accelerated not only repeated alterations in leadership but also four unsuccessful non-violent coup attempts in 1995, 1998, 2003 and 2009. Sao Tome and Principe's economy mainly relies on the agricultural production, while we must not ignore that it is highly dependent on imports of fuels, consumer goods, food and the majority of manufactured goods (Alao, 1999; Chabal, 1996; CIA Factbook/Sao Tome and Principe, 2019; De Medeiros Carvalho, 2015; Encyclopedia "Domi", Vol. 24; Encyclopedia "The Counselor of the Young", Vol. 8; Galli, 1987; Hamilton, 1991a and 1991b; Moser, 1999; Penvenne, 2003; Vasileiou, 2019f).

The last step of our historical overview is Timor-Leste and apart from highly interesting, its history is undeniably complicated.

On November 28, 1975, East Timor indeed declared itself independent from Portugal, while only nine days later it was invaded and occupied by Indonesian forces. In July 1976, East Timor was incorporated into Indonesia. In the context of the following two decades, approximately 100,000 to 250,000 people lost their lives in terms of a far from efficacious attempt for the coveted peace restoration. We also have to mention that, back in 1999, in terms of a UN-supervised popular referendum that took place in August, a huge majority of Timor-Leste's people voted for independence from Indonesia. In the following three weeks the nightmare began. More specifically, a number of anti-independence Timorese militias, which were systematically organized and backed by the Indonesian military actually started a huge retribution campaign. In brief, we have to mention that around 1,400 Timorese were killed and 300,000 people were forced into western Timor as refugees by the militias. What is more, the biggest part of the country's infrastructure was ruined. It is not difficult to realize that at that particular time the country was in total chaos. The positive feature was that on September 20, 1999, Australian-led peacekeeping troops managed to stop the violence. Finally, on May 20, 2002, Timor-Leste was internationally recognized as an independent state (CIA Factbook/Timor-Leste, 2019; Encyclopedia "Domi", Vol. 12 and 27; Encyclopedia "The Counselor of the Young", Vol. 5; Purnell History of the 20th Century, 1968, Vol 5; World History 1, 1990).

We would like to believe that this brief aforementioned analysis has managed to efficaciously provide the reader with a sufficient general view with regard to the six PALOP-TL member states.

We opted to avoid the presentation of too many details due to the fact that we wanted this analysis to be something like an introduction to the following meticulous examination which takes place via the systematic use of numerous quantitative data.

So, in the next paragraphs, a critical presentation with respect to a number of interesting geographical, economic and trade information with regard to the six PALOP-TL member countries takes place. Relevant data are being painstakingly scrutinized and we remain sure that this analysis will offer the reader the opportunity to become more familiar with these six highly interesting in far too many senses countries.

As we will notice, the data presented indisputably cover a wide range of tremendously notable issues and the spectrum of our analysis is incontrovertibly broad. Nonetheless, we would like to believe that the specific method on which our analysis has relied manages to eventually simplify everything in the most serviceable manner. And we surely have to mention again that this quantitative data research method is to a certain extent similar to the one we have already used in terms of some of our previous books (Vasileiou, 2013a, 2014a, 2015, 2017c, 2018c, 2019a, 2019b, 2019f, 2019h, 2019j and 2019k).

Angola is again the initial step of our scrutiny. It is the largest and most populated PALOP-TL member state. Its capital city is Luanda and other significant cities are N'dalatando, Lubango, Huambo, Lobito and Kuito.

Its total area is 1,246,700 sq km [Country Comparison to the World (CCW): 24], its population 30,355,880 (July 2018 est.) and its coastline 1,600 km. Angola's natural resources are a) uranium,

b) petroleum, c) bauxite, d) diamonds, e) gold, f) iron ore, g) feldspar, h) phosphates and i) copper. The percentage of its agricultural land reaches 47.5% (2016 est.) and that of forest 46.3% (2016 est.). Its irrigated land is 860 sq km (2014). Angola's GDP (purchasing power parity) was $193.6 bn (2017 est.), $198.6 bn (2016 est.) and $203.9 bn (2015 est.) (data are in 2017 dollars-CCW: 65). Its GDP real growth rate was -2.5% (2017 est.), -2.6% (2016 est.) and 0.9% (2015 est.) (CCW: 209), while its GDP (official exchange rate) is $126.5 bn (2017 est.). Moreover, its GDP per capita (PPP) was $6,800 (2017 est.), $7,200 (2016 est.) and $7,600 (2015 est.) (data are in 2017 dollars-CCW: 160). In terms of Gross National Saving, that was 28.6% of GDP (2017 est.), 24.5% of GDP (2016 est.) and 28.5% of GDP (2015 est.) (CCW: 37). We also have to add that Angola's GDP composition by sector of origin is a) industry 61.4% (2011 est.), b) services 28.4% (2011 est.) and c) agriculture 10.2% (2011 est.) (CIA Factbook/Angola, 2019; Encyclopedia "Domi", Vol. 1; Encyclopedia "The Counselor of the Young", Vol. 1; Purnell History of the 20th Century, 1968, Vol 1 and 6; Vasileiou, 2019f; World History 1, 1990).

Angola's agricultural products are a) bananas, b) fish, c) forest products, d) sugarcane, e) livestock, f) coffee, g) plantains, h) sisal, i) vegetables, j) corn, k) tobacco, l) cotton and m) cassava (manioc, tapioca). Its industries comprise a) petroleum, b) diamonds, c) ship repair, d) textiles, e) iron ore, f) sugar, g) phosphates, h) tobacco products, i) feldspar, j) brewing,

k) bauxite, l) food processing, m) uranium and gold, n) fish processing, o) cement and p) basic metal products. What is more, its industrial production growth rate is 2.5% (2017 est.) (CCW: 115) and its labor force 12.51 million (2017 est.) (CCW: 46). Angola's labor force by occupation can be categorized as follows: a) agriculture 85%, b) industry 15% (2015 est.) and c) industry and services 15% (2003 est.). Its unemployment rate is 6.6% (2016 est.) (CCW: 97) and its population below poverty line 36.6% (2008 est.). Apart from that, Angola's public debt was 65% of GDP (2017 est.) and 75.3% of GDP (2016 est.) (CCW: 59). Its inflation rate (consumer prices) was 29.8% (2017 est.) and 30.7% (2016 est.) (CCW: 222). Its external debt was $42.08 bn (31/12/2017 est.) and $27.14 bn (31/12/2016 est.) (CCW: 71) (CIA Factbook/Angola, 2019; Encyclopedia "Domi", Vol. 1; Encyclopedia "The Counselor of the Young", Vol. 1; Vasileiou, 2019f; World History 1, 1990).

Angola's exports amounted to $33.07 bn (2017 est.) and $31.03 bn (2016 est.) (CCW: 60). Its imports accounted for $19.5 bn (2017 est.) and $13.04 bn (2016 est.) (CCW: 78). In addition to that, its foremost exports partners are a) China (61.2%), b) India (13%) and c) the USA (4.2%) (2017). As far as its exports commodities are concerned, these are a) diamonds, b) cotton, c) sisal, d) timber, e) crude oil, f) fish and fish products, g) coffee and h) refined petroleum products. In terms of its most notable imports partners, these are a) Portugal (17.8%), b) China (13.5%), c) the USA (7.4%), d) South Africa

(6.2%), e) Brazil (6.1%) and f) the UK (4%) (2017). Its imports commodities are a) machinery and electrical equipment, b) vehicles and spare parts, c) food, d) textiles, e) medicines and f) military goods (CIA Factbook/Angola, 2019; Vasileiou, 2019f).

Angola's crude oil production is 1.593 million bbl/day (2018 est.) (CCW: 14). Its crude oil exports are 1,782 million bbl/day (2015 est.) (CCW: 7) but its imports are zero (2015 est.) (CCW: 88). What is more, its crude oil proved reserves are 9.523 bn bbl (1/1/18 est.) (CCW: 16). In terms of the production of refined petroleum products, this is 53,480 bbl/day (2015 est.) (CCW: 80), while their consumption is 130,000 bbl/day (2016 est.) (CCW: 72). The exports in terms of refined petroleum products are 30,340 bbl/day (2015 est.) (CCW: 62) and the imports 111,600 bbl/day (2015 est.) (CCW: 50). Angola's natural gas production is 3.115 bn cu m (2017 est.) (CCW: 55) and its consumption 821.2 million cu m (2017 est.) (CCW: 95). Its natural gas imports are zero (2017 est.) and its exports are 3.993 bn cu m (2017 est.) (CCW: 33). Finally, its proved reserves, always in terms of natural gas are 308.1 bn cu m (1/1/2018 est.) (CCW: 36) and its carbon dioxide emissions from energy consumption 20.95 million Mt (2017 est.) (CCW: 85) (CIA Factbook/Angola, 2019; Vasileiou, 2019f).

Following the presentation of the abovementioned data, we would like to make a number of comments. First and foremost, in terms of Angola's GDP (purchasing power parity) a reduction can be observed from 2015 to 2017 and in the same period there was also a decrease with regard to its GDP per capita (PPP).

Apart from that, in terms of its GDP composition by sector of origin (2011 est.), industry is by far on top of the list. Furthermore, with respect to Angola's public debt (as percentage of GDP), a reduction took place between 2016 and 2017. On the contrary, in the context of its external debt, a huge rise can be noticed between 31/12/2016 and 31/12/2017. What is more, we must not disregard the truly important fact that Angola's inflation rate (consumer prices) was decreased between 2016 and 2017. Finally, as regards its exports partners (2017), China is by far in the first position, while in terms of its imports partners (2017) Portugal ranks first.

Our analysis continues with Guinea-Bissau. Its capital city is Bissau and other important cities are Bafata, Gabu, Bissora, Bolama and Cacheu.

Its total area is 36,125 sq km (CCW: 138), its population 1,833,247 (July 2018 est.) and its coastline 350 km. Its natural resources are a) fish, b) unexploited petroleum deposits, c) timber, d) limestone, e) granite, f) phosphates, g) clay and h) bauxite. The percentage of its agricultural land reaches 44.8% (2011 est.) and that of forest 55.2% (2011 est.). Its irrigated land is only 250 sq km (2012). Guinea-Bissau's GDP (purchasing power parity) was $3.171 bn (2017 est.), $2.994 bn (2016 est.) and $2.817 bn (2015 est.) (data are in 2017 dollars-CCW: 188). Furthermore, its GDP real growth rate was 5.9% (2017 est.), 6.3% (2016 est.) and 6.1% (2015 est.) (CCW: 36). Guinea-Bissau's GDP (official exchange rate) is $1.35 bn (2017 est.) and its GDP per capita (PPP) was $1,900 (2017 est.), $1,800 (2016 est.) and $1,700 (2015 est.) (data are in 2017 dollars-CCW: 212). In terms of Gross National Saving, that was 8.6% of GDP (2017 est.), 10.1% of GDP (2016 est.) and 10.5% of GDP (2015 est.) (CCW: 168). Guinea-Bissau's GDP composition by sector of origin is a) agriculture 50% (2017 est.), b) services 36.9% (2017 est.) and c) industry 13.1% (2017 est.). Its agricultural products are a) rice, b) cashew nuts, c) palm kernels, d) fish, e) timber, f) beans, g) corn, h) peanuts, i) cotton and j) cassava (manioc, tapioca). Moreover, its industries comprise a) beer, b) agricultural products processing and c) soft drinks. Its industrial production growth rate is 2.5% (2017 est.) (CCW: 117) and its labor force 731,300 (2013 est.) (CCW: 151). Its labor force by occupation can be categorized as follows: a) agriculture 82%, and b) industry and services 18% (2000 est.). We must also add that its population below poverty line is 67% (2015 est.) (CIA Factbook/Guinea-Bissau, 2019; Encyclopedia "Domi", Vol. 7; Encyclopedia "The Counselor of the Young", Vol. 3; World History 1, 1990).

Guinea-Bissau's public debt was 53.9% of GDP (2017 est.) and 57.9% of GDP (2016 est.) (CCW: 87). Its inflation rate (consumer prices) was 1.1% (2017 est.) and 1.5% (2016 est.) (CCW: 60). Its external debt was $1.095 bn (31/12/2010 est.) and $941.5 million (31/12/2000 est.) (CCW: 164). Apart from that, Guinea-Bissau's exports amounted to $328.1 million (2017 est.) and $278.6 million (2016 est.) (CCW: 185).

Its imports accounted for $283.5 million (2017 est.) and $136.5 million (2016 est.) (CCW: 205). Its foremost exports partners are a) India (67.1%) and b) Vietnam (21.1%) (2017). As far as its exports commodities are concerned, these are a) peanuts, b) fish, c) shrimp, d) raw and sawn lumber, e) palm kernels and f) cashews. In terms of its most notable imports partners, these are a) Portugal (47.8%), b) Senegal (12.1%), c) China (10.4%), d) Netherlands (8.1%) and e) Pakistan (5.4%) (2017). Its imports commodities are a) machinery and transport equipment, b) petroleum products and c) foodstuffs. Guinea-Bissau's crude oil production, exports, and imports are zero bbl/day (2018 est. for production and 2015 est. for exports and imports). Its proved reserves, always in terms of crude oil, are also zero bbl (1/1/2018 est.). In the context of the production of refined petroleum products, this is zero bbl/day (2015 est.) and their consumption 2,700 bbl/day (2016 est.) (CCW: 190). The exports in terms of refined petroleum products are zero bbl/ day (2015 est.), whereas the imports 2,625 bbl/day (2015 est.) (CCW: 186). Moreover, Guinea-Bissau's natural gas production, consumption, imports and exports are zero cu m (2017 est.). Finally, its proved reserves, always in terms of natural gas are also zero cu m (1/1/2014 est.) and its carbon dioxide emissions from energy consumption are 397,900 Mt (2017 est.) (CCW: 188) (CIA Factbook/Guinea-Bissau, 2019).

As we can see, with regard to Guinea Bissau's GDP (purchasing power parity), an increase can be observed from 2015 to 2017.

What is more, in the same period, there was also a raise with regard to its GDP per capita (PPP). Apart from that, as regards Guinea Bissau's GDP composition by sector of origin (2017 est.), agriculture can be found in the first position. Also, with respect to its public debt (as percentage of GDP), a reduction was noticed between 2016 and 2017.

On the contrary, in the context of its external debt, we can observe a rise between 31/12/2000 and 31/12/2010. Furthermore, its inflation rate (consumer prices) was decreased between 2016 and 2017. Finally, in terms of its exports partners (2017), India is by far in the first position, while in terms of its imports partners (2017) Portugal ranks first.

Cape Verde is the third PALOP-TL member state we thoroughly examine. Its capital city is Praia and other noteworthy cities are Mindelo, Santa Maria, Cova Figueira, Santa Cruz and Pedra Badejo.

Its total area is 4,033 sq km (CCW: 176), its population 568,373 (July 2018 est.) (CCW: 173) and its coastline 965 km. Its natural resources are a) basalt rock, b) salt, c) gypsum, d) clay, e) limestone and f) kaolin. The percentage of its agricultural land reaches only 18.6% (2011 est.) and that of forest 21% (2011 est.). Its irrigated land is just 35 sq km (2012). Cape Verde's GDP (purchasing power parity) was $3.777 bn (2017 est.), $3.631 bn (2016 est.) and $3.468 bn (2015 est.) (data are in 2017 dollars-CCW: 182). Also, it is worth mentioning that its GDP real growth rate was 4% (2017 est.), 4.7% (2016 est.)

and 1% (2015 est.) (CCW: 75). What is more, Cape Verde's GDP (official exchange rate) is $1.776 bn (2017 est.) and its GDP per capita (PPP) was $7,000 (2017 est.), $6,800 (2016 est.) and $6,600 (2015 est.) (data are in 2017 dollars-CCW: 157). In terms of Gross National Saving, that was 32.4% of GDP (2017 est.), 34.8% of GDP (2016 est.) and 35.6% of GDP (2015 est.) (CCW: 25). Apart from that, Cape Verde's GDP composition by sector of origin is a) services 73.7% (2017 est.), b) industry 17.5% (2017 est.) and c) agriculture 8.9% (2017 est.). Cape Verde's agricultural products are a) bananas, b) fish, c) peanuts, d) sugarcane, e) beans, f) coffee, g) sweet potatoes and h) corn. Its industries comprise a) fish processing, b) salt mining, c) food and beverages, d) ship repair and e) shoes and garments. Its industrial production growth rate is 2.9% (2017 est.) (CCW: 107) and its labor force 196,100 (2007 est.) (CCW: 174) (CIA Factbook/Cape Verde, 2019; Encyclopedia "The Counselor of the Young", Vol. 8; World History 2, 1990).

Cape Verde's unemployment rate is 9% (2017 est.) and this percentage was identical in the previous year as well (CCW: 131). Its population below poverty line is 30% (2000 est.). Its public debt was 125.8% of GDP (2017 est.) and 127.6% of GDP (2016 est.) (CCW: 8). Its inflation rate (consumer prices) was 0.8% (2017 est.) and -1.4% (2016 est.) (CCW: 39). Its external debt was $1.713 bn (31/12/2017 est.) and $1.688 bn (31/12/2016 est.) (CCW: 155). Cape Verde's exports amounted to just $189 million (2017 est.) and $148.4 million (2016 est.) (CCW: 190).

Its imports accounted for $836.1 million (2017 est.) and $687.3 million (2016 est.) (CCW: 188). In addition to that, its foremost exports partners are a) Spain (45.3%), b) Portugal (40.3%) and c) Netherlands (8.1%) (2017). As far as its exports commodities are concerned, these are a) shoes, b) fuel (re-exports), c) fish, d) garments and e) hides. In terms of its most notable imports partners, these are a) Portugal (43.9%), b) Spain (11.6%), c) Netherlands (6.1%) and d) China (6.1%) (2017). Its imports commodities are a) transport equipment, b) fuels, c) foodstuffs and d) industrial products. Cape Verde's crude oil production (2018 est.) and its crude oil exports and imports (2015 est.) are zero bbl/day. Its crude oil proved reserves are also zero bbl (1/1/2018 est.). With regard to the production of refined petroleum products, this is zero bbl/day (2015 est.), while their consumption is 5,600 bbl/day (2016 est.) (CCW: 173). The exports in terms of refined petroleum products are zero bbl/day (2015 est.), whereas the imports are 5,607 bbl/day (2015 est.) (CCW: 166). Cape Verde's natural gas production, consumption, imports and exports are zero cu m (2017 est.). Finally, its proved reserves, always in terms of natural gas are also zero cu m (1/1/2016 est.) and its carbon dioxide emissions from energy consumption 867,800 Mt (2017 est.) (CCW: 172) (CIA Factbook/Cape Verde, 2019).

As we can easily conclude, it terms of Cape Verde's GDP (purchasing power parity) an increase can be observed from 2015 to 2017. Moreover, in the same period, there was also a rise with regard to its GDP per capita (PPP).

Apart from that, in terms of its GDP composition by sector of origin (2017 est.), services are by far in the first position. Furthermore, with respect to its public debt (as percentage of GDP), there was also a reduction between 2016 and 2017 while in the context of its external debt a raise can be observed between 31/12/2016 and 31/12/2017.

Emphasis must also be placed on the fact that its inflation rate (consumer prices) was increased between 2016 and 2017, while its unemployment rate remained identical in both 2016 and 2017. Finally, with regard to its exports partners (2017), Spain ranks first closely followed by Portugal, while in terms of its imports partners (2017) Portugal is by far in the first position.

Mozambique is the fourth step of our analysis. It is the second largest, as well as the second most populated PALOP-TL member state after Angola. Its capital city is Maputo and other notable cities are Matola, Beira, Nampula, Chimoio and Nacala.

Its total area is 799,380 sq km (CCW: 36), its population 27,233,789 (July 2018 est.) and its coastline 2,470 km, much longer compared to that of all PALOP-TL members. Its natural resources are a) titanium, b) coal, c) hydropower, d) graphite, e) tantalum and f) natural gas. The percentage of its agricultural land reaches 56.3% (2011 est.) and that of forest 43.7% (2011 est.). Its irrigated land is 1,180 sq km (2012). Mozambique's GDP (purchasing power parity) was $37.09 bn (2017 est.), $35.76 bn (2016 est.) and $34.46 bn (2015 est.) (data are in

2017 dollars-CCW: 122). Its GDP real growth rate was 3.7% (2017 est.), 3.8% (2016 est.) and 6.6% (2015 est.) (CCW: 91). Mozambique's GDP (official exchange rate) is $12.59 bn (2017 est.) and its GDP per capita (PPP) was $1,300 (2017 est.), $1,200 (2016 est.) and $1,200 (2015 est.) (data are in 2017 dollars-CCW: 222). In terms of Gross National Saving, that was 16.8% of GDP (2017 est.), -1.2% of GDP (2016 est.) and 5% of GDP (2015 est.) (CCW: 123). Also, its GDP composition by sector of origin is a) services 56.8% (2017 est.), b) agriculture 23.9% (2017 est.) and c) industry 19.3% (2017 est.). Mozambique's agricultural products are a) citrus and tropical fruits, b) cashew nuts, c) poultry, d) sugarcane, e) beef, f) sunflowers, g) potatoes, h) sisal, i) tea, j) corn, k) coconuts, l) cotton and m) cassava (manioc, tapioca) (CIA Factbook/Mozambique, 2019; Encyclopedia "Domi", Vol. 18; Encyclopedia "The Counselor of the Young", Vol. 7; Purnell History of the 20th Century, 1968, Vol 1, 2 and 6; Vasileiou, 2019f; World History 2, 1990).

Its industries comprise a) petroleum products, b) aluminum, c) chemicals (fertilizer, soap, paints), d) textiles, e) glass, f) asbestos, g) beverages, h) tobacco, i) cement and j) food. Its industrial production growth rate is 4.9% (2017 est.) (CCW: 61) and its labor force 12.9 million (2017 est.) (CCW: 45). Its labor force by occupation can be categorized as follows: a) agriculture 74.4%, b) services 21.7% and c) industry 3.9% (2015 est.). Its unemployment rate was 24.5% (2017 est.) and 25% (2016 est.) (CCW: 196). Its population below poverty line is

46.1% (2015 est.). Moreover, Mozambique's public debt was 102.1% of GDP (2017 est.) and 121.6% of GDP (2016 est.) (CCW: 15). Its inflation rate (consumer prices) was 15.3% (2017 est.) and 19.2% (2016 est.) (CCW: 212). Its external debt was $10.91 bn (31/12/2017 est.) and $10.48 bn (31/12/2016 est.) (CCW: 110). Mozambique's exports amounted to $4.725 bn (2017 est.) and $3.328 bn (2016 est.) (CCW: 111). Its imports accounted for $5.223 bn (2017 est.) and $4.733 bn (2016 est.) (CCW: 124). In addition to that, its foremost exports partners are a) India (28.1%), b) the Netherlands (24.4%) and c) South Africa (16.7%) (2017) (CIA Factbook/Mozambique, 2019; Vasileiou, 2019f).

As far as its exports commodities are concerned, these are a) aluminum, b) cotton, c) prawns, d) timber, e) citrus, f) cashews, g) sugar and h) bulk electricity. In terms of its most notable imports partners, these are a) South Africa (36.8%), b) China (7%), c) UAE (6.8%), d) India (6.2%) and e) Portugal (4.4%) (2017). Its imports commodities are a) machinery and equipment, b) vehicles, c) foodstuffs, d) textiles, e) metal products, f) fuel and g) chemicals. Mozambique's crude oil production, exports, and imports are zero bbl/day (2018 est. for production and 2015 est. for exports and imports). Its proved reserves, always in terms of crude oil, are also zero bbl (1/1/2018 est.). In terms of the production of refined petroleum products, this is also zero (2015 est.) but their consumption is 26,000 bbl/day (2016 est.) (CCW: 128). The exports in terms of refined petroleum products are zero (2015 est.), whereas the imports are 25,130 bbl/day (2015 est.) (CCW: 107). Mozambique's natural gas production is 6.003 bn cu m (2017 est.) (CCW: 47) and its consumption 1.841 bn cu m (2017 est.) (CCW: 84). Mozambique's natural gas imports are zero (2017 est.), while its exports are 4.162 bn cu m (2017 est.) (CCW: 32). Finally, its proved reserves, always in terms of natural gas are 2.832 trillion cu m (1/1/2018 est.) (CCW: 13) and its carbon dioxide emissions from energy consumption 11.12 million Mt (2017 est.) (CCW: 102) (CIA Factbook/Mozambique, 2019; Vasileiou, 2019f).

Following the data presentation, we can conclude that in terms of Mozambique's GDP (purchasing power parity) a raise can be observed from 2015 to 2017. What is more, there was also an increase with regard to its GDP per capita (PPP) from 2016 to 2017.

We have to add that in terms of its GDP composition by sector of origin (2017 est.), services are by far on top of the list. Apart from that, with respect to its public debt (as percentage of GDP), a reduction can be noticed between 2016 and 2017 whereas in the context of its external debt, a rise can be observed between 31/12/2016 and 31/12/2017.

Furthermore, we must not ignore the fact that its inflation rate (consumer prices) was decreased between 2016 and 2017 and its unemployment rate was also reduced in the same period. As regards its exports partners (2017), India ranks first closely followed by the Netherlands. Finally, in terms of its imports partners (2017) South Africa is by far first.

Our critical scrutiny continues with Sao Tome and Principe, which is the smallest PALOP-TL member country and, concomitantly, the least populated one. Its capital city is Sao Tome and other significant cities are Santo Amaro, Neves, Santana, Trindade and Santa Cruz.

Its total area is solely 964 sq km (CCW: 185), its population just 204,454 (July 2018 est.) (CCW: 184) and its coastline 209 km. Its natural resources are hydropower and fish. The percentage of its agricultural land reaches 50.7% (2011 est.) and that of forest 28.1% (2011 est.). Its irrigated land is only 100 sq km (2012). Sao Tome and Principe's GDP (purchasing power parity) was $686 million (2017 est.), $660.4 million (2016 est.) and $633.9 million (2015 est.) (data are in 2017 dollars-CCW: 208). Its GDP real growth rate was 3.9% (2017 est.), 4.2% (2016 est.) and 3.8% (2015 est.) (CCW: 83). What is more, São Tomé and Príncipe's GDP (official exchange rate) is $393 million (2017 est.). Its GDP per capita (PPP) was $3,200 (2017 est.), $3,200 (2016 est.) and $3,100 (2015 est.) (data are in 2017 dollars-CCW: 191). In terms of Gross National Saving, that was 18.7% of GDP (2017 est.), 21% of GDP (2016 est.) and 19.3% of GDP (2015 est.) (CCW: 25). We have to add that Sao Tome and Principe's GDP composition by sector of origin is a) services 73.4% (2017 est.), b) industry 14.8% (2017 est.) and c) agriculture 11.8% (2017 est.) (CIA Factbook/Sao Tome and Principe, 2019; Encyclopedia "Domi", Vol. 24; Encyclopedia "The Counselor of the Young", Vol. 8; Vasileiou, 2019f).

Its agricultural products are a) bananas, b) fish, c) coconuts, d) palm kernels, e) beans, f) coffee, g) cinnamon, h) copra, i) pepper, j) papayas, k) poultry and l) cocoa. Moreover, Sao Tome and Principe's industries comprise a) fish processing, b) soap, c) light construction, d) timber, e) beer and f) textiles. Its industrial production growth rate is 5% (2017 est.) (CCW: 57) and its labor force 72,600 (2007 est.) (CCW: 186). Its labor force by occupation can be categorized as follows: a) agriculture 26.1%, b) industry 21.4% and c) services 52.5% (2014 est.). Its unemployment rate was 12.2% (2017 est.) and 12.6% (2016 est.) (CCW: 163). Furthermore, Sao Tome and Principe's population below poverty line is 66.2% (2009 est.). Its public debt was 88.4% of GDP (2017 est.) and 93.1% of GDP (2016 est.) (CCW: 27) Its inflation rate (consumer prices) was 5.7% (2017 est.) and 5.4% (2016 est.) (CCW: 182). Its external debt was $292.9 million (31/12/2017 est.) and $308.5 million (31/12/2016 est.) (CCW: 185) (CIA Factbook/Sao Tome and Principe, 2019; Encyclopedia "Domi", Vol. 24; Encyclopedia "The Counselor of the Young", Vol. 8; Vasileiou, 2019f).

Sao Tome and Principe's exports amounted to just $15.6 million (2017 est.) and $9.31 million (2016 est.) (CCW: 215). Its imports accounted for $127.7 million (2017 est.) and $119.1 million (2016 est.) (CCW: 212). Its foremost exports partners are a) Guyana (43.7%), b) Germany (23.6%), c) Portugal (6%), d) the Netherlands (5.5%) and e) Poland (4.4%) (2017). As far as its exports commodities are concerned, these are

a) cocoa (68%), b) copra, c) coffee and d) palm oil (2010 est.). In terms of its most notable imports partners, these are a) Portugal (54.7%), b) Angola (16.5%) and c) China (5.6%) (2017). Its imports commodities are a) machinery and electrical equipment, b) petroleum products and c) food products. Sao Tome and Principe's crude oil production (2018 est.) and its crude oil exports (2015 est.) and imports (2015 est.) are zero bbl/day. Furthermore, its crude oil proved reserves (1/1/2018) are also zero bbl. In terms of the production of refined petroleum products, this is zero bbl/day (2017 est.), whereas their consumption is 1,000 bbl/day (2016 est.) (CCW: 206). The exports in terms of refined petroleum products are zero bbl/day (2015 est.), while the imports 1,027 bbl/day (2015 est.) (CCW: 202). Moreover, Sao Tome and Principe's natural gas production, consumption, imports and exports are zero cu m (2017 est.). Finally, its proved reserves, always in terms of natural gas are also zero cu m (1/1/2014 est.) and its carbon dioxide emissions from energy consumption are 148,100 Mt (2017 est.) (CCW: 204) (CIA Factbook/Sao Tome and Principe, 2019; Vasileiou, 2019f).

In order to summarize some of the findings with regard to Sao Tome and Principe, first of all we have to note that in terms of its GDP (purchasing power parity), there was an increase from 2015 to 2017. What is more, in terms of its GDP per capita (PPP), between 2015 and 2016 a raise also took place, while between 2016 and 2017 no alteration whatsoever could be noticed.

In terms of its GDP composition by sector of origin (2017 est.), services are by far in the first position. Also, with respect to its public debt (as percentage of GDP), there was a reduction between 2016 and 2017 while in the context of its external debt there was also a decrease between 31/12/2016 and 31/12/2017.

Moreover, we must not forget that its inflation rate (consumer prices) was increased between 2016 and 2017, but its unemployment rate was reduced in the same period. As regards its exports partners (2017), Guyana ranks first and this comes as a surprise. Finally, in terms of its imports partners (2017), Portugal is by far in the first position.

Timor-Leste is the sixth and final step of our examination and as we have already mentioned it is the sole PALOP-TL member not located in Africa. However, it is worth noting that despite its enormous distance from the other five PALOP-TL countries, it remains an outstandingly significant member for numerous reasons. Its capital city is Dili, and other important cities are Maliana, Suai, Likisa, Aileu and Lospalos.

Its total area is 14,874 sq km (CCW: 160), its population 1,321,929 (July 2018 est.) (CCW: 156) and its coastline 706 km. Its natural resources are a) natural gas, b) marble, c) gold, d) petroleum and e) manganese. Its agricultural land is only 25.1% (2011 est.) and that of forest 49.1% (2011 est.). Its irrigated land is 350 sq km (2012). Timor-Leste's GDP (purchasing power parity) was $7.426 bn (2017 est.), $7.784 bn (2016 est.) and $7.391 bn (2015 est.) (data are in 2017 dollars-CCW: 166).

Also, its GDP real growth rate was -4.6% (2017 est.), 5.3% (2016 est.) and 4% (2015 est.) (CCW: 216). Timor-Leste's GDP (official exchange rate) is $2.775 bn (2017 est.), while its GDP per capita (PPP) was $6,000 (2017 est.), $6,400 (2016 est.) and $6,200 (2015 est.) (data are in 2017 dollars-CCW: 164). We have to add that Timor-Leste's GDP composition by sector of origin is a) industry 56.7% (2017 est.), b) services 34.4% (2017 est.) and c) agriculture 9.1% (2017 est.). Its agricultural products are a) bananas, b) rice, c) sweet potatoes, d) vanilla, e) cassava (manioc, tapioca), f) coffee, g) corn, h) mangoes, i) soybeans and j) cabbage, while its industries comprise a) soap manufacturing, b) printing, c) woven cloth and d) handicrafts. Its industrial production growth rate is 2% (2017 est.) (CCW: 133) and its labor force 286,700 (2016 est.) (CCW: 164) (CIA Factbook/Timor-Leste, 2019; Encyclopedia "Domi", Vol. 12 and 27; Encyclopedia "The Counselor of the Young", Vol. 5; Purnell History of the 20th Century, 1968, Vol 5; World History 1, 1990).

Timor-Leste's unemployment rate was 4.4% (2014 est.) and 3.9% (2010 est.) (CCW: 60). Furthermore, its population below poverty line is 41.8% (2014 est.). Apart from that, its public debt was 3.8% of GDP (2017 est.) and 3.1% of GDP (2016 est.) (CCW: 206). Its inflation rate (consumer prices) was 0.6% (2017 est.) and -1.3% (2016 est.) (CCW: 34). Its external debt was $311.5 million (31/12/2014 est.) and $687 million (31/12/2013 est.) (CCW: 184). Timor-Leste's exports amounted to just $16.7 million (2017 est.) and $18 million (2015 est.) (CCW: 214).

What is more, its imports accounted for $681.2 million (2017 est.) and $558.6 million (2016 est.) (CCW: 192). As far as its exports commodities are concerned, these are a) coffee, b) oil, c) marble and d) sandalwood, while it is worth mentioning that there is potential with regard to vanilla exports. Its imports commodities are a) gasoline, b) machinery, c) kerosene and d) food. Timor-Leste's crude oil production is 33,000 bbl/day (2018 est.) (CCW: 60). Its crude oil exports are 62,060 bbl/day (2015 est.) (CCW: 39), while its imports are zero bbl/day (2015 est.). Its crude oil proved reserves are also zero bbl (1/1/2018 est.) (CIA Factbook/Timor-Leste, 2019).

Moreover, in terms of the production of refined petroleum products, this is also zero bbl/day (2015 est.), whereas their consumption is 3,500 bbl/day (2016 est.) (CCW: 186). The exports in terms of refined petroleum products are zero bbl/day (2015 est.), while the imports are 3,481 bbl/day (2015 est.) (CCW: 182). Timor-Leste's natural gas production is 5.776 bn cu m (2017 est.) (CCW: 48) and its consumption zero cu m (2017 est.). Its natural gas imports are also zero cu m (2017 est.), while its exports are 5.776 bn cu m (2017 est.) (CCW: 27). Finally, its proved reserves, always in terms of natural gas are 200 bn cu m (1/1/2006 est.) (CCW: 42) and its carbon dioxide emissions from energy consumption 533,400 Mt (2017 est.) (CCW: 184) (CIA Factbook/Timor-Leste, 2019).

As we can see, with respect to Timor-Leste's GDP (purchasing power parity) a reduction can be observed from 2016 to 2017, which followed the raise that took place from 2015 to 2016.

Furthermore, as regards its GDP per capita (PPP), an increase from 2015 to 2016 and a reduction from 2016 to 2017 can actually be noticed. Apart from that, in terms of its GDP composition by sector of origin (2017 est.), industry is by far in the first position.

It is also worth mentioning that as far as its public debt (as percentage of GDP) is concerned, a rise was observed from 2016 to 2017 while in the context of its external debt we can observe a huge reduction between 31/12/2013 and 31/12/2014. Finally, its inflation rate (consumer prices) was increased between 2016 and 2017, while its unemployment rate was also raised between 2010 and 2014.

We would like to believe that the meticulous presentation of all the aforesaid historical and geographical information accompanied by a number of interesting quantitative data has enabled the reader to become familiar with the six PALOP-TL member states in a truly satisfactory manner.

In the following chapter we aim to achieve three main targets. Firstly, we attempt a critical comparison of the six PALOP-TL member countries, using the data which have already been conscientiously presented in this chapter.

Our dominant aim is to methodically summarize the foremost findings and we strongly believe that this comparison will offer the reader the opportunity to draw a number of interesting conclusions, clarify any dark points and perhaps continue the research from the point we have stopped.

Secondly, we critically focus on some incontestably noteworthy journal articles which have managed to provide us with outstandingly interesting information not only in terms of politics and economics but also with respect to history, culture and civilization in general.

Thirdly, we painstakingly concentrate on a specific range of certain plans and actions with a view to a more functional cooperation between PALOP-TL and the EU. It goes without saying that such collaboration has already been successful and it is gradually improving. Therefore, any further attempt for a deeper and perhaps even more fruitful combined effort by the two sides in question is irrefutably worth mentioning.

As we will see, numerous highly notable steps have in reality taken place and we try to highlight them in the best possible manner. Nonetheless, as always, time will be the only judge as regards whether these truly ambitious objectives will become a reality precisely the way they have been planned.

CHAPTER **2**

A CRITICAL COMPARISON BETWEEN PALOP-TL MEMBERS AND THE COOPERATION WITH THE EUROPEAN UNION

This chapter has been divided into three equally important parts. In the first, we attempt a comparative scrutiny of the six PALOP-TL member countries using the data we have meticulously presented in the context of the previous chapter.

In order to be more precise we have to note that in terms of the previous chapter our dominant objective was to examine the six member states separately. On the contrary, here, a brief comparative analysis takes place in a systematic as well as simplified manner.

We remain certain that such a method of analysis will make it easier for the reader to efficaciously deepen his knowledge with regard to the six member countries in order afterwards to be capable of drawing his personal conclusions. We strongly believe that in this case numbers indeed tell the truth and reveal a lot about the six PALOP-TL member states.

In the second part, we critically focus on a number of truly notable articles which have managed to provide us with highly interesting information not only in terms of politics and economics but also with regard to history and culture. More specifically, as we have already mentioned in the introduction, we meticulously concentrate on the work by Alao, Chabal, De Medeiros Carvalho, Galli, Hamilton and Moser.

Finally, in the third part, we painstakingly concentrate on the planning and actions of PALOP-TL and the EU in order to achieve a better cooperation which is highly probable to be much more beneficial for all sides with respect not only to the present but also to the future.

It is true that the EU keeps promoting and encouraging that kind of relations all over the world in a truly efficacious method within its outstandingly significant international cooperation and development context. Its principal target is the sufficient creation of specific partnerships for change in terms of developing countries (Vasileiou, 2013a, 2014a, 2015, 2017c, 2018c, 2019a, 2019b, 2019f, 2019h, 2019j and 2019k).

At this point our critical comparison begins. First of all, as regards the total area and the population of the six PALOP-TL member states, it is not difficult to conclude that Angola and Mozambique can be found in the first two positions. On the contrary, the smallest member country is Sao Tome and Principe which is also the least populated one.

Moreover, as far as the percentage of agricultural land is

concerned, the highest can be observed in Mozambique (56.3%) (2011 est.), while the lowest in Cape Verde (18.6%) (2011 est.). With regard to the longest coastline, this is that of Mozambique (2,470 km), whereas the shortest one is that of Sao Tome and Principe (209 km). In terms of irrigated land, the largest can be observed in Mozambique (1,180 sq km) (2012) and the smallest in Cape Verde (35 sq km) (2012).

With respect to Gross National Saving (2017 est.) Cape Verde (32.4% of GDP) ranks first. Guinea-Bissau (8.6% of GDP) can be found in the last position, while there is no available data for Timor-Leste. As we can easily notice, the difference between the first and the last country is 23.8 percentage points which is incontrovertibly huge. In terms of GDP (purchasing power parity) (2017 est.-data are in 2017 dollars), rather expectedly, Angola is by far in the first position ($193.6 bn), while Sao Tome and Principe ($686 million) is the last one.

Attention must be paid to the fact that in the context of GDP real growth rate (2017 est.), Guinea-Bissau (5.9%) ranks first, while it is also worth mentioning that the difference between the first and the last [(Timor-Leste (-4.6%)]] is not at all insignificant. Moreover, as far as GDP (official exchange rate) (2017 est.) is concerned, Angola ($126.5 bn) ranks first, while São Tomé and Príncipe ($393 million) can be observed in the last position.

Apart from that, with respect to GDP per capita (PPP) (2017 est.-data are in 2017 dollars), Cape Verde ($7,000) can be found in the first position, while Mozambique ($1,300) is the last one. Nonetheless, the truly staggering feature is the huge difference between these two countries. Additionally, special emphasis must be placed on the significant difference between the three first countries and the three last ones.

What is more, in terms of industrial production growth rate (2017 est.), São Tomé and Príncipe (5%) ranks first, closely followed by Mozambique (4.9%). Timor-Leste (2%) can be observed in the last position, but what we need to highlight is the notable difference between the first two countries and the rest.

As far as unemployment rate is concerned, the list is the following: a) Mozambique (24.5%) (2017 est.) and (25%) (2016 est.), b) Sao Tome and Principe (12.2%) (2017 est.) and (12.6%) (2016 est.), c) Cape Verde (9%) (2017 est.) and (9%) (2016 est.), d) Angola (6.6%) (2016 est.) and e) Timor-Leste (4.4%) (2014 est.) and (3.9%) (2010 est.).

Unfortunately, we could not discover any data whatsoever with regard to Guinea-Bissau. However, if we compare the data we possess, we can observe that Timor-Leste is characterized by the lowest unemployment rate, while Mozambique by the highest. Moreover, the difference between Mozambique and the second highest (Sao Tome and Principe) is incontestably enormous and such a detail is undeniably worth mentioning.

With regard to population below poverty line, the list is as follows: a) Guinea-Bissau (67%) (2015 est.), b) Sao Tome and

Principe (66.2%) (2009 est.), c) Mozambique (46.1%) (2015 est.), d) Timor-Leste 41.8% (2014 est.), e) Angola (36.6%) (2008 est.) and f) Cape Verde (30%) (2000 est.).

It is not difficult to notice that Guinea-Bissau is on top, closely followed by Sao Tome and Principe. Nonetheless, the general conclusion is that the percentage in all the six countries is incontrovertibly high. Such an element is indeed disappointing and incontrovertibly calls for rapid and sufficient action.

In terms of public debt (2017 est.), Cape Verde (125.8% of GDP) is by far in the first position. However, the truly astonishing feature is the outstandingly low percentage of Timor-Leste (3.8% of GDP). With respect to inflation rate (consumer prices) (2017 est.), Angola is first with an enormous percentage, almost double compared to the second Mozambique. Timor-Leste can be found in the last position, but the interesting element is the tremendously low percentage of Guinea-Bissau, Cape Verde and Timor-Leste.

It is really worth mentioning that Angola's inflation rate is around 29 percentage points higher compared to Guinea-Bissau, Cape Verde and Timor-Leste and such a parameter must not go unnoticed for numerous quite obvious reasons.

Apart from that, as regards external debt (31/12/2017 est.), the list is as follows: a) Angola ($42.08 bn), b) Mozambique ($10.91 bn), c) Cape Verde ($1.713 bn), d) Guinea-Bissau ($1.095 bn) (31/12/2010 est.), e) Timor-Leste ($311.5 million) (31/12/2014 est.) and f) Sao Tome and Principe ($292.9 million).

As expected, Angola is on top with a huge difference compared to the second Mozambique. Furthermore, in the context of exports (2017 est.), again, rather expectedly, Angola ($33.07 bn) is in the first position with a significant difference from the second Mozambique. Sao Tome and Principe ($15.6 million) is in the last position.

Nonetheless, the truly interesting feature is the enormous difference between the exports of the first two countries and the rest. Apart from that, with regard to imports (2017 est.), Angola ranks first ($19.5 bn), while Sao Tome and Principe ($127.7 million) can be found in the last position. The foremost conclusion we can draw after examining both imports and exports is that in terms of Angola and Guinea-Bissau, their exports are more than their imports. And in the case of Angola, the difference reaches $13.57 bn, which is a far from insignificant amount.

It goes without saying that such a detail is irrefutably staggering and it is not difficult to understand why. Furthermore, with respect to imports' partners (2017), Portugal ranks first in the cases of Angola, Guinea-Bissau, Cape Verde and Sao Tome and Principe. In terms of exports' partners (2017), India is first in the cases of Mozambique and Guinea-Bissau and second in the case of Angola. Nevertheless, a truly astounding fact is that Guyana ranks first in the case of Sao Tome and Principe and with a significantly high percentage which reaches 43.7%. Regrettably, no data for Timor-Leste could be discovered with respect to either its imports' or its exports' partners.

Finally, with regard to GDP composition by sector of origin (2017 est.), industry ranks first in Angola (61.4%) (2011 est.) and Timor-Leste (56.7%). Services can be observed in the first position in Cape Verde (73.7%) and Sao Tome and Principe (73.4%) and Mozambique (56.8%). On the contrary, agriculture can be noticed in the first position only in Guinea-Bissau (50%).

We remain certain that the abovementioned comparative analysis has incontrovertibly offered the reader the chance to draw some notable conclusions with regard to the numerous differences that exist between the six PALOP-TL member countries. Nonetheless, we can irrefutably argue that despite all these differences (some of which are more or less anticipated) PALOP-TL is a well-balanced and homogeneous group at least for the time being.

As we have already mentioned, according to our research in general, the journal articles in English dealing with PALOP-TL or PALOP we have actually discovered are indeed limited and such a phenomenon in a sense strengthens our argument that these countries have not yet received the attention they deserve (Vasileiou, 2013a, 2014a, 2015, 2017c, 2018c, 2019a, 2019b, 2019f, 2019h, 2019j and 2019k).

Nevertheless, it is true that some outstandingly notable journal articles irrefutably exist and provide us with some really interesting information not only with respect to politics and economics but also as regards history and culture.

More specifically, Galli (1987) painstakingly focuses on the food crisis and the Socialist State in Lusophone Africa. In the context of her tremendously significant article she claims that the fiscal, commercial and exchange rate policies combined with the response of the biggest part of rural producers to them were the foremost causes that managed to define the specific trade and production conditions between 1974 and 1984 in the context of Lusophone Africa.

We also have to note that Galli does not ignore several other notable factors such as a) the depressed state with regard to international commodity markets, b) an externally-provoked destabilization and c) the utmost significance of drought that have incontrovertibly resulted in not only reduced agricultural exports but also an evident food shortage.

What is more, she clearly states that, always at the time her article was being authored, Lusophone Africa's agriculture policies were actually reflecting the early colonial mentality toward peasants under the pretence of socialist policy.

In addition to that, Galli notes that postcolonial states had actually continued taking advantage of peasant labor either via state marketing organizations or through private plantations and colossal state farms. In other cases, they left peasants mainly alone to do whatever they wanted providing very little towards an enhancement with regard to their working conditions, while also slowing the marketing progress. What is more, they managed to keep concentrating resources on export agriculture to the damage of food production.

Furthermore, Galli strongly argues that to the oppressive colonial legacy, Angola, Cape Verde, Mozambique and Sao Tome and Principe added the model of the highly mechanized state farm as a producer of not only food but also exports. This is a highly notable argument that reveals a lot about that particular period and it goes without saying that in the context of her article Galli raises some tremendously serious issues.

De Medeiros Carvalho (2015) attempts to systematically compare the highly notable evolution with regard to Japan's and China's foreign policies to the Lusophone Africa. His article meticulously concentrates on the era after 2000. De Medeiros Carvalho claims that it is highly probable for Japan's development edge over China with respect to the so-called "aid-model" approach towards PALOP members to be under threat.

Following our conscientious scrutiny of this article, we can effectively draw the conclusion that the abovementioned element incontrovertibly results in numerous questions with regard to China's altering aid pattern, which can effectively be regarded as a raising amount of "soft" assistance towards PALOP members outside of investment and trade relations which can indeed be characterized as in agreement with the Japanese aid practices.

It goes without saying that both China and Japan are tremendously interested as regards PALOP members, hence, De Medeiros Carvalho via his painstaking examination manages to discover numerous complementarities in terms of the two countries' assistance allocation to PALOP members.

Good examples are a) the significant empowerment in the context of local communities systematically promoted by Japanese's aid focus on human-security projects and grassroots and b) poverty elimination, taking into account the sectoral diversity as regards the Chinese assistance.

In the context of another attention-grabbing article, Hamilton (1991b) critically focuses on a highly notable linguistic aspect. In order to be more precise we have to note that he underlines the end of Portugal's colonial empire, which incontrovertibly raises two important questions.

The first concerns the (perhaps up to a point uncertain) future of the Portuguese language in Africa and, indeed in the world beyond, while the second is about whether the literatures of these new African countries keep being written mainly in Portuguese. It goes without saying that Hamilton deals with an incontrovertibly crucial subject which must not be underestimated at all.

Chabal (1996) meticulously examines the prospects for democracy in Lusophone Africa. More specifically, he conducts a meticulous scrutiny on the history of the PALOP countries, focusing on some of the most important political evolutions and providing the reader with numerous interesting details emphasizing the most adverse political crises.

Chabal clearly argues that the governments which managed to eventually gain power at independence in the context of the five PALOP countries supported socialism despite the fact that a number of significant differences could be observed with respect to their ideological position.

Moser (1999) meticulously focuses on some of the neglected or forgotten authors of Lusophone Africa. Through his article, he attempts to convince younger scholars and their advisers to actually dare to go beyond the already well-known ones such as a) the Mozambicans Bernardo Mia Couto and Jose Craveirinha and b) the Angolans Carlos Pepetela and Luandino Vieira and explore other outstandingly notable but probably less-known authors of Lusophone Africa.

It is worth mentioning that Moser painstakingly highlights the significance of numerous other authors from the literatures of Lusophone Africa. More specifically, he mentions Mario Antonio Fenandes de Oliveira, Orlando de Albuquerque, Antonio Aurelio Goncalves, Henrique Teixeira de Sousa, Gloria de Sant'Anna, Rui (Correia) Knopfli, Fausto Duarte, Helder Proenca and Aldo (do) Espirito Santo.

All of them have incontestably contributed a great deal to the literature of Lusophone Africa and it would not be an exaggeration to state that the systematic scrutiny of their work can irrefutably provide the readers with diamonds in terms of literature and culture in general. We also have to underline that Moser's selection with regard to the abovementioned authors was strictly personal, always according to his own preferences.

Alao (1999) critically concentrates on the development of Lusophone Africa's literary magazines. He points out that despite the several extended (and irrefutably devastating we would add) armed conflicts that took place in this area and incontrovertibly caused disorder with respect to its general cultural and social life, at the time his article was being authored, the literary press had actually not suffered any significant decline as far as production was concerned.

On the contrary, Alao strongly argues that if it was possible for a survey to take place, the findings would show that both in numerical terms and in proportion to the population it actually represented, Lusophone Africa had in reality created a higher amount of literary magazines compared to numerous other African zones.

Of course, we have to mention that this article was published in 1999 and it is highly probable that some things might be slightly different now. Nonetheless, if we take into account that a) the population of Cape Verde, Guinea-Bissau and Sao Tome and Principe was extremely limited and b) apart from the armed conflicts, all the countries of Lusophone Africa were ceaselessly experiencing adverse economic problems, we can incontrovertibly draw the conclusion that Alao's findings are tremendously encouraging.

What is more, at a specific point in the context of his article, Alao in a sense questions himself if the fact that the literary press did not suffer any decline in production was thanks to the several (and indeed harsh we would surely add) armed conflicts.

Following our meticulous scrutiny with regard to the history of these countries, we will not disagree with this argument. Another interesting point by Alao is that at the time his article was being authored, it was infrequent in Lusophone Africa to discover writers who did not commence their literature publication in literary periodicals. The conclusion is that in the context of Lusophone Africa, literary periodicals were the most "accessible" means of communication available to potential participants as regards literary creation.

Indisputably, we remain in position to argue that all the abovementioned articles clearly highlight several notable details as far as PALOP countries are concerned. Lusophone Africa is a truly fascinating area of study in far too many senses and it comes as no surprise that the Portuguese impact is still evident in linguistic terms. Hence, in the near future, we expect to come across more books or journal articles methodically dealing with these specific countries.

Apart from its internal actions, PALOP-TL ceaselessly operates with a view to an even more fruitful relationship with the EU. More specifically, PALOP-TL and the EU keep moving towards an enhanced cooperation in a highly methodical manner and this is an element that incontrovertibly calls for further analysis for numerous quite obvious reasons for both the present and the future.

Therefore, in the following paragraphs we attempt to a) systematically conduct a detailed scrutiny with respect to

PALOP-TL's fundamental aims and b) critically examine its incessant attempts for an even more functional collaboration with the EU.

We are all aware of the fact that the EU keeps promoting similar cooperative relations with numerous regions and regional groups all over the globe. The majority of these relations are indubitably constructive, while in the context of all of them, the primary target is the benefit of all sides without exceptions (Vasileiou, 2013a, 2014a, 2015, 2017c, 2018c, 2019a, 2019b, 2019f, 2019h, 2019j and 2019k).

It goes without saying that difficulties of all kinds are unavoidable, especially if we take into account that some of the (developing) countries that form part of these groups have indeed experienced (or keep experiencing) numerous serious political or economic tribulations, crises or destabilizations (Vasileiou, 2013a, 2014a, 2015, 2017c, 2018c, 2019a, 2019b, 2019f, 2019h, 2019j and 2019k).

It is true that relevant examples are far too many and unambiguously highlight the inevitable difficulties of those specific countries to enter into the coveted road of progress. Of course we do not imply that progress is impossible but it is highly probable to take too long in order to eventually become a reality (Vasileiou, 2013a, 2014a, 2015, 2017c, 2018c, 2019a, 2019b, 2019f, 2019h, 2019j and 2019k).

Nonetheless, the important feature is that in the majority of cases all sides try to collaborate in the best possible manner towards a satisfactory present and a much more promising tomorrow, even if in some cases the results cannot be regarded as very encouraging (Vasileiou, 2013a, 2014a, 2015, 2017c, 2018c, 2019a, 2019b, 2019f, 2019h, 2019j and 2019k).

Back in 1975, after their coveted national independence eventually became a reality, Angola, Cape Verde, Guinea-Bissau, Mozambique and Sao Tome and Principe (PALOP) managed to successfully join the tremendously notable partnership agreement of the ACP countries with the European Community (EC) and that was an undeniably gigantic step towards a more heartening future.

Moreover, we are aware of the fact that from the mid-1980s onwards, PALOP governments actually commenced a number of interesting thoughts and actions so as to systematically recognize common cooperation programs with the EC. Undeniably, that was a major initiative towards a far more functional collaboration and as we will notice in the following paragraphs, despite a number of anticipated and in a sense inevitable difficulties this much-needed cooperation managed to gradually flourish in a truly efficacious manner. What is more, we strongly believe that such a significant feature simplified a number of outstandingly noteworthy procedures and in a sense offered additional impetus towards a far more efficient joint action.

It is indeed worth mentioning that the EU keeps promoting in a highly methodical manner the so-called "South-South" cooperation among the six Portuguese speaking countries from the African Caribbean and Pacific (ACP) group. In our opinion, it would not be an exaggeration to argue that PALOP can be regarded as one of the most harmonious and well-balanced ACP groupings (Alao, 1999; Chabal, 1996; De Medeiros Carvalho, 2015; European Commission/PALOP-TL, 2019; Galli, 1987; Hamilton, 1991a and 1991b; Moser, 1999; Penvenne, 2003; Vasileiou, 2013a, 2014a, 2015, 2017c, 2018c, 2019a, 2019b, 2019f, 2019h, 2019j and 2019k).

What is more, we surely have to underline that the systematic cooperation between the five African countries has its roots back in the 1970s. We must also add that the EU has actually supported the group since 1992. This undeniably notable collaboration is based on the Cotonou Agreement and financed via the European Development Fund (EDF) (Alao, 1999; Chabal, 1996; De Medeiros Carvalho, 2015; European Commission/ PALOP-TL, 2019; Galli, 1987; Hamilton, 1991a and 1991b; Moser, 1999; Penvenne, 2003; Vasileiou, 2013a, 2014a, 2015, 2017c, 2018c, 2019a, 2019b, 2019f, 2019h, 2019j and 2019k).

More specifically, in the context of the 10th EDF, the PALOP-TL allocation was of €33.1 million, while we must also mention that the EU support rather expectedly gave priority to the always neuralgic area of good governance. This included a) public services, b) democratization and human rights, c) economic governance and d) rule of law (European Commission/PALOP-TL, 2019; Vasileiou, 2015 and 2019j).

It is not difficult to realize that all four abovementioned subcategories are equally significant and in a sense complementary. All four can indubitably contribute a great deal towards the efficacious functioning of this cooperation and cover perhaps the most fundamental aspects of any suchlike collaboration apart from this one (Vasileiou, 2013a, 2014a, 2015, 2017c, 2018c, 2019a, 2019b, 2019f, 2019h, 2019j and 2019k).

It is true that in terms of a number of our previous books, we have indeed scrutinized numerous similar cooperations and the conclusion drawn is that good governance with all its relevant parameters, factors and components is a priceless element towards more evident signs of progress either in the near or the distant future (Vasileiou, 2013a, 2014a, 2015, 2017c, 2018c, 2019a, 2019b, 2019f, 2019h, 2019j and 2019k).

According to our hitherto conducted research, not only for this book but also for some of our previous ones, we remain perfectly sure that EU's experience accompanied by its well-conducted planning clearly identified the need for an increased emphasis on good governance in the context of that specific period (Vasileiou, 2013a, 2014a, 2015, 2017c, 2018c, 2019a, 2019b, 2019f, 2019h, 2019j and 2019k).

In terms of the 11th EDF (2014-20), the cooperation programming between PALOP-TL and the EU is presented and analyzed in the "Regional Indicative Programme for PALOP and Timor Leste". What is more, we have to argue that the abovementioned program actually foresees an initial envelope of €30 million and manages to sufficiently combine the new (and of course equally significant if not more) priorities and the program's revised governance structure agreed by the EU representatives and the PALOP-TL member states in the context of the annual ministerial meeting held in Luanda in March 2014 (European Commission/PALOP-TL, 2019; Vasileiou, 2015 and 2019j).

In the following and final chapter, the most significant concluding remarks are being methodically presented. The already achieved targets, the still-existing problems and the most ambitious future steps are being summarized in the best possible manner always with a view to a coherent understanding that can somehow lead to a perhaps more efficacious further research.

It is rather obvious that accurate future predictions are totally impossible but this does not prevent us from systematically emphasizing some of the most interesting prospects. This cooperation can already be characterized as successful, therefore, a more promising tomorrow cannot be excluded.

CHAPTER 3

CONCLUDING REMARKS

PALOP-TL comprises five African countries and Timor-Leste which is located in Southeast Asia. Angola and Mozambique are by far the two largest and most populated members, but in our opinion this element does not have a negative impact on the group's balance in general.

Following our hitherto conducted research, we have eventually reached the conclusion that all six countries are characterized by strong historical, linguistic and cultural bonds and this is one of the foremost reasons for the success and the durability of this group.

Apart from the slightly problematic situation in terms of politics and economics with regard to PALOP-TL member states, it is worth highlighting that Lusophone Africa has always had a unique charm in terms of language, literature and culture.

Thus, its meticulous examination in the context of these fields is incontrovertibly fascinating.

It would not be an exaggeration to state that PALOP can irrefutably be regarded as one of the most functional ACP groupings and it is not difficult to realize the momentousness of such a factor. The cooperation between the five African countries has its roots back in the 1970s while we also have to note that the EU has systematically supported the group since 1992.

Indubitably, numerous differences in terms of both politics and economics among the group's members are evident, but the important thing is that such an element does not hamper (at least for the time being) either the group's satisfactory operation or its multidimensional future planning. It is also true that all PALOP-TL member countries have repeatedly experienced numerous adverse political tribulations including in some cases severe destabilizations, armed conflicts and civil wars. And we are all aware of the fact that the impact of such situations in a developing country is totally different compared to that in a developed one.

Nonetheless, it is truly worth mentioning that these tribulations did not have an adverse effect on the PALOP-TL group as a whole, at least as far as we are concerned. And what we mean is that they did not manage to destroy the group, which still remains alive and kicking. It goes without saying that such an element is undoubtedly worth mentioning and we truly hope that in the future PALOP-TL will remain as strong as these days.

In addition to the aforesaid thorny problems, we must also add the global economic and financial instability that currently exists all over the world and unavoidably affects not only PALOP-TL as a whole but also its individual member states.

What is more, another crucial parameter that incontestably has to be highlighted is the huge distance between some of the six member states, which, however, has not created thus far any serious problems with regard to PALOP-TL's smooth operation.

Nonetheless, despite the widespread and to a certain extend justified optimism, a number of burning issues still remain. According to the data we have collected, a highly negative feature, in terms of all the PALOP-TL member states without a single exception is the outstandingly high percentage of population below poverty line. Regrettably, this ranges from 30% to 67% and such an element unquestionably calls for increased attention and rapid action. We strongly believe that the reduction of these percentages indubitably remains a core priority no matter how difficult this achievement may be.

Two were the principle objectives of this book. The first was the meticulous presentation of the profiles of the six PALOP-TL member states, followed by an extensive comparative analysis in order for a number of interesting conclusions to be effectively drawn.

Therefore, a wealth of notable quantitative data accompanied by numerous important details with regard to geography, history and politics of the six member states was painstakingly analyzed in the context of an attempt to provide the reader with the most recent information with respect to these countries. We would like to believe that this presentation took place in a coherent and well-conducted manner with a view to the best possible understanding.

The second objective was the conscientious scrutiny with regard to PALOP-TL's ceaseless attempts to significantly enhance its truly multidimensional cooperation with the EU. And as we have noticed, this collaboration is gradually flourishing, providing us with numerous encouraging messages with regard to a brighter future.

It would not be an exaggeration to argue that these days economic instability is evident all over the globe. Hence, any attempts whatsoever towards a highly systematic economic cooperation which, inter alia, will be indeed beneficial for developing countries must be incontestably highlighted and praised in the most pronounced way.

Additionally, we strongly believe that the specific method on which our analysis has been based has in reality managed to efficaciously shed light on a number of slightly or perhaps totally unknown issues.

According to our hitherto conducted research, one of the conclusions drawn is that PALOP-TL has been somewhat neglected in the context of the current literature and we mean books and journal articles in English.

It would not be an exaggeration to note that such a feature

has indeed surprised us, being aware of the group's increasing notability not only in politicoeconomic terms but also with regard to history, culture and civilization in general. We would like to believe that this book will somehow serve as a starting point or perhaps as a serviceable compass towards a more systematic research with respect to this group.

We really hope that our examination has managed to convince the reader about the several crucial steps that have so far taken place towards a more promising tomorrow. What is more, we remain sure that the significance of PALOP-TL will be increased in the near future and we hope that such an element will attract the attention of even more scholars to efficaciously conduct more and perhaps better research as regards this undoubtedly fascinating in far too many senses group.

BIBLIOGRAPHY

Alao, George (1999), "The Development of Lusophone Africa's Literary Magazines", *Research in African Literatures*, 30 (1), pp. 169-183.

Chabal, Patrick (1996), "The Prospects for Democracy in Lusophone Africa", *Portuguese Studies*, 12, pp. 185-200.

CIA Factbook/Angola (2019), "The World Factbook: Africa: Angola", The World Factbook 2019 (Washington, DC: Central Intelligence Agency, 2019), available at https://www.cia.gov/library/publications/the-world-factbook/geos/print_ao.html (accessed on 24/10/19).

CIA Factbook/Cape Verde (2019), "The World Factbook: Africa: Cabo Verde", The World Factbook 2019 (Washington, DC: Central Intelligence Agency, 2019), available at https://www.cia.gov/library/publications/the-world-factbook/geos/print_cv.html (accessed on 24/10/19).

CIA Factbook/Guinea-Bissau (2019), "The World Factbook: Africa: Guinea-Bissau", The World Factbook 2019 (Washington, DC: Central Intelligence Agency, 2019), available at https://www.cia.gov/library/publications/the-world-factbook/geos/print_pu.html (accessed on 24/10/19).

CIA Factbook/Mozambique (2019), "The World Factbook: Africa: Mozambique", The World Factbook 2019 (Washington, DC: Central Intelligence Agency, 2019), available at https://www.cia.gov/library/publications/the-world-factbook/geos/print_mz.html (accessed on 24/10/19).

CIA Factbook/Sao Tome and Principe (2019), "The World Factbook: Africa: Sao Tome and Principe", The World Factbook 2019 (Washington, DC: Central Intelligence Agency, 2019), available at https://www.cia.gov/library/publications/the-world-factbook/geos/print_tp.html (accessed on 24/10/19).

BIBLIOGRAPHY

CIA Factbook/Timor-Leste (2019), "The World Factbook: East Asia/Southeast Asia: Timor-Leste", The World Factbook 2019 (Washington, DC: Central Intelligence Agency, 2019), available at https://www.cia.gov/library/publications/the-world-factbook/geos/print_tt.html (accessed on 24/10/19).

De Medeiros Carvalho, Pedro Miguel Amakasu Raposo (2015), "China's and Japan's Foreign Aid Policies vis-à-vis Lusophone Africa", *Africa Spectrum*, 50 (3), pp. 49-79.

Encyclopedia "Domi" (in Greek), Vol. 1 (Athens: "Domi" Publications).

Encyclopedia "Domi" (in Greek), Vol. 7 (Athens: "Domi" Publications).

Encyclopedia "Domi" (in Greek), Vol. 12 (Athens: "Domi" Publications).

Encyclopedia "Domi" (in Greek), Vol. 18 (Athens: "Domi" Publications).

Encyclopedia "Domi" (in Greek), Vol. 24 (Athens: "Domi" Publications).

Encyclopedia "Domi" (in Greek), Vol. 27 (Athens: "Domi" Publications).

Encyclopedia "The Counselor of the Young" (original name: Ο Σύμβουλος των Νέων) (in Greek), Vol. 1 (Athens: Atlas Publications).

Encyclopedia "The Counselor of the Young" (original name: Ο Σύμβουλος των Νέων) (in Greek), Vol. 3 (Athens: Atlas Publications).

Encyclopedia "The Counselor of the Young" (original name: Ο Σύμβουλος των Νέων) (in Greek), Vol. 5 (Athens: Atlas Publications).

Encyclopedia "The Counselor of the Young" (original name: Ο Σύμβουλος των Νέων) (in Greek), Vol. 7 (Athens: Atlas Publications).

Encyclopedia "The Counselor of the Young" (original name: Ο Σύμβουλος των Νέων) (in Greek), Vol. 8 (Athens: Atlas Publications).

BIBLIOGRAPHY

European Commission/PALOP-TL (2019), "International Cooperation and Development: PALOP-TL", available at https://ec.europa.eu/europeaid/regions/africa/palop-tl_en (accessed on 2/11/19). Content owned by the EU on this website is licensed under the Creative Commons Attribution 4.0 International (CC BY 4.0) license.

Galli, Rosemary E. (1987), "The Food Crisis and the Socialist State in Lusophone Africa", *African Studies Review*, 30 (1), pp. 19-44.

Hamilton, Russell G. (1991a), "Lusofonia, Africa, and Matters of Languages and Letters", *Hispania*, 74 (3), pp. 610-617.

Hamilton, Russell G. (1991b), "Lusophone Literature in Africa: Lusofonia, Africa, and Matters of Languages and Letters", *Callaloo*, 14 (2), pp. 324-335.

Moser, Gerald M. (1999), "Neglected or Forgotten Authors of Lusophone Africa", *World Literature Today*, 73 (1), pp. 19-22.

Penvenne, Jeanne Marie (2003), "Special Issue: Colonial Encounters between Africa and Portugal: An Introduction", *The International Journal of African Historical Studies*, 36 (1), pp. 1-6.

Purnell History of the 20th Century (1968), Vol. 1 (BPC Publishing Ltd, exclusive rights to translation into Greek and circulation in Greece "Chrysos Typos" S.A.).

Purnell History of the 20th Century (1968), Vol. 2 (BPC Publishing Ltd, exclusive rights to translation into Greek and circulation in Greece "Chrysos Typos" S.A.).

Purnell History of the 20th Century (1968), Vol. 5 (BPC Publishing Ltd, exclusive rights to translation into Greek and circulation in Greece "Chrysos Typos" S.A.).

BIBLIOGRAPHY

Purnell History of the 20th Century (1968), Vol. 6 (BPC Publishing Ltd, exclusive rights to translation into Greek and circulation in Greece "Chrysos Typos" S.A.).

Vasileiou, Ioannis (2013a), *European Unification-A Process of Convergence, or Divergence?* (in Greek) (Athens: Historical Quest).

Vasileiou, Ioannis (2013b), "1980-1999, European Union: The Years of Expansion and Enlargement", *From Hitler's New Europe to Merkel's Eurozone* (in Greek), Vol. 1, Historical Archive of Ependytis, pp. 76-95.

Vasileiou, Ioannis (2014a), *European Unification-A Process of Convergence, or Divergence?* (2nd Edition-Special Edition for Universities) (in Greek) (Athens: Historical Quest).

Vasileiou, Ioannis (2014b), *The Present and Future of the Agricultural Policy of the European Union* (in Greek) (Athens: Historical Quest).

Vasileiou, Ioannis (2015), *The Foreign and Security Policy of the European Union-A Critical Approach* (in Greek) (Athens: Historical Quest).

Vasileiou, Ioannis (2017a), *Climate Change: Manageable Problem or Slow Death of the Planet? EU Role and Actions until 2050-The Impact on Greece* (in Greek) (Athens: Historical Quest).

Vasileiou, Ioannis (2017b), *Economic Crisis, Employment and Social Affairs in the European Union-Proposals and Actions to Combat Unemployment* (in Greek) (Athens: Historical Quest).

Vasileiou, Ioannis (2017c), *EU Budget-Issues About the Allocation and Redistribution of Resources in the EU* (in Greek) (Athens: Historical Quest).

Vasileiou, Ioannis (2017d), *European Union and Energy-The Route Towards 2050-Thoughts, Ideas and Conclusions* (in Greek) (Athens: Historical Quest).

BIBLIOGRAPHY

Vasileiou, Ioannis (2017e), *The European Union Expansion Into Space* (in Greek) (Athens: Historical Quest).

Vasileiou, Ioannis (2018a), *Climate Change: Manageable Problem or Slow Death of the Planet? European Union Role and Actions until 2050-The Impact on Greece* (The Greek edition translated into English) (Independently Published/Amazon KDP-Available through Amazon).

Vasileiou, Ioannis (2018b), *Enterprises in the EU: Monopolies-Cartels-State Aid-Competition Rules* (in Greek) (Athens: Historical Quest).

Vasileiou, Ioannis (2018c), *European Union Budget-Issues About the Allocation and Redistribution of Resources in the European Union* (The Greek edition translated into English) (Independently Published/Amazon KDP-Available through Amazon).

Vasileiou, Ioannis (2018d), *The European Union Expansion Into Space* (The Greek edition translated into English) (Independently Published/Amazon KDP-Available through Amazon).

Vasileiou, Ioannis (2019a), *Canada and Mexico: Trade Relations with the European Union: Towards an Even More Functional Cooperation* (Independently Published/Amazon KDP-Available through Amazon).

Vasileiou, Ioannis (2019b), *China-India-ASEAN-Gulf Region: Trade Relations with the European Union* (The Greek edition translated into English) (Independently Published/Amazon KDP-Available through Amazon).

Vasileiou, Ioannis (2019c), *Economic Crisis, Employment and Social Affairs in the European Union-Proposals and Actions to Combat Unemployment* (The Greek edition translated into English) (Independently Published/Amazon KDP-Available through Amazon).

BIBLIOGRAPHY

Vasileiou, Ioannis (2019d), *Enterprises in the EU-Monopolies-Cartels-State Aid-Competition Rules* (The Greek edition translated into English) (Independently Published/Amazon KDP-Available through Amazon).

Vasileiou, Ioannis (2019e), *European Union and Energy-The Route towards 2050-Thoughts, ideas and conclusions* (The Greek edition translated into English) (Independently Published/Amazon KDP-Available through Amazon).

Vasileiou, Ioannis (2019f), *European Union Trade: Trade Relations with Central Africa, the Southern African Development Community, Central America, the Andean Community and South Korea* (Independently Published/Amazon KDP-Available through Amazon).

Vasileiou, Ioannis (2019g), *Health in the European Union: Member States-Agencies-Policies: Thoughts and Suggestions for the Present and the Future* (Independently Published/ Amazon KDP-Available through Amazon).

Vasileiou, Ioannis (2019h), *Mercosur: Past, Present and Future of Integration in South America-Trade and Economic Relations with the European Union* (Independently Published/Amazon KDP-Available through Amazon).

Vasileiou, Ioannis (2019i), Taxation and Fraud Prevention in the European Union: Lessons Learned and Future Prospects (Independently Published/Amazon KDP-Available through Amazon).

Vasileiou, Ioannis (2019j), *The Foreign and Security Policy of the European Union: A Critical Approach* (2nd fully revised edition) (The first edition was published in Greek in 2015) (Independently Published/Amazon KDP-Available through Amazon).

BIBLIOGRAPHY

Vasileiou, Ioannis (2019k), *Vietnam and New Zealand: The Profiles: History-Trade-Economy* (Independently Published/ Amazon KDP-Available through Amazon).

World History 1 (1990), Educational Greek Encyclopedia (in Greek) (Athens: Ekdotiki Athinon).

World History 2 (1990), Educational Greek Encyclopedia (in Greek) (Athens: Ekdotiki Athinon).

IOANNIS VASILEIOU

BIOGRAPHY

Ioannis Vasileiou was born in Athens in 1978. In 2001, he was awarded his Ptychio (equivalent to Bachelor's degree) in Political Science and Public Administration from the University of Athens (Greece). In 2003, he was awarded his first Master's degree (International Political Economy) from the University of Warwick (UK). In 2005, he was awarded his second Master's degree (International Economic Management) from the University of Birmingham (UK). In 2011, he was awarded his PhD from the University of Birmingham (UK) with specialization in the economic and political aspects of the European Union's Regional Policy. Since 2011, he has been conducting academic research on issues related to the European Union and international politics and economics.

9 781711 652245